Grand Canyon

and

Other Selected Poems

Amil Quayle   *1974*

Grand Canyon

and

Other Selected Poems

Amil Quayle

Foreword

by

Brad Dimock

*For My Brother Henry
1946-2007*

Black Star Press

Black Star Press
2236 A Street
Lincoln, NE 68502
slfbsp@gmail.com

Distributed by
Henry's Fork Books
P. O. Box 1, St. Anthony, ID 83445
208-521-2744
quayamil@isu.edu

Copyright © 2009 by Amil Quayle
All rights reserved. Printed in the United States of America.
First Edition, Second Printing
ISBN: 978-1-887810-00-5

Edited by Julie Thomson

The following publications previously published these poems:
Alternatives: An American Poetry Anthology, Greg Kuzma, ed.,
    Best Cellar Press, 1987, "The Grand Canyon"
The Boatman's Quarterly Review (The News), "The Grand Canyon,"
    "Old Boatmen Revised," "Shawn," "Sons and Rivers" &
    "Stairways"
Four Hands Full (Pocatello Blend 13), Blue Scarab Press, 2004,
    "The Death by Drowning of My Brother Cheddy" &
    "Stairways"
Hungarian Horse Association Newsletter, "Sister Horse"
Literary Review, "Stairways"
The Midwest Quarterly, "Empyrean, Nebraska"
Northern Lights, "A Memory"
Redneck Review, "The Wood Carver"

Other books by Amil Quayle:
Pebble Creek, A Slow Tempo Press, 1993
Four Hands Full (Pocatello Blend 13), Blue Scarab Press, 2004

CONTENTS

Foreword by Brad Dimock	vii
Grand Canyon	1
Go There	2
Matisse Was Obsessed with Light	3
Sons and Rivers	4
Grandson and Grand Canyon	5
Ode to Shorty Burton at Upset Rapid	7
Old Boatmen Revised	8
An Invocation	11
A boatman falls asleep in the Grand Canyon 1969	12
Stairways	13
Brautigan Farewell 1985	15
Big Montana Sky	16
The Mules at Phantom Ranch	17
Sawtooth Range	18
The Death of Ed Abbey	19
Shawn	20
My Sons, There Were Other Times	21
For All My Grandchildren	23
Digging Postholes	25
My Father's House	26
The Octogenarian	28
A Memory	30
Our Mother's Garden	32
Boy and Dog on the Dam	34
The Death by Drowning of My Brother Cheddy	38
Riding Icebergs on the Snake River	40
The Beet Dump	42
A Good Portion of My Tongue Lies Buried with the Lincoln School	43
Music Appreciation and President John F. Kennedy	46
Poetry as Metaphor	47
A Short History of World War II for the Oldest of Five Brothers	48
Across the Mountains with Brother Henry the Trucker	49
Grandpa Died in a Sheepcamp	53
Silence and the Coming of Spring	54
100 Teams	55

The Tallest Stone in the Cemetery	56
Saddle Musings	57
A Woman	59
When the Sun Went Backward in the Sky	60
The Wood Carver	62
Alex	64
Cowboy Poet	66
Write a Poem about Me	68
Sister Horse	69
The Sleeping Coyote	71
To the Bobcats I Knew in 1977	72
The Coal Trains	73
Leaves from the Hackberry Tree	74
Walking with Alvin	76
At 50	78
Three Loaves	80
The Surprise Snow	82
A Walk in the February Snow	83
Tater, the Invincible Dachshund	84
Two Spring Rains	87
After Twelve Years in Nebraska	89
A Man Can't Hide	89
Defining the Loss	90
At Night in the Trailer	92
The Simple Joy of Finding a Twelve-Foot Tall Sunflower Growing in My Front Yard from a Seed of Unknown Origin after Returning from a Summer in the Mountains	93
The Milford Times	95
Empyrean, Nebraska	96
Milo Field Goodbye	97
In Lincoln, Nebraska with Carl Jung and Robert Service at Midnight	98
The Old Man and the Sea	101
Isaac	103
The Day Comes	105
To those who believe	106
Sancho Panza and the McDonald's Happy Meal	108
Imagine	110
List of Illustrations	112

Foreword

I know Amil Quayle mostly through osmosis. He had left Grand Canyon shortly before I arrived in the early 1970s. His name was still in the air. Many of his friends and boatmates soon became mine: the Quist brothers, Stu Reeder, Ken Sleight. I worked on boats with the words "Quayle Expeditions" peeking through worn silver paint. I packed many a trip out of his old warehouse in Green River. Stories of Amil always came up, and his name was always spoken with respect and admiration, with the love for a good man.

Amil had left the river for Nebraska for reasons his friends understood poorly. Something about family, tradition, working the land. They missed him sorely. What wasn't apparent to me then–it is now–was that a portion of Amil's soul got stuck here. A large chunk still swirls in the muddy currents and leaves an ache in his chest. You feel it in his poems.

Me, I just kind of stumbled into river running–first at college, then as a swamper on commercial trips, then as a guide on the big motor rigs. The place did not capture me at first. Like many, I came, was amazed and moved, yet could probably easily have moved on if chance had opened other doors. But the summer job drew me back year after year. Slowly, silently, and solidly, the hook set inside me.

What is it about Grand Canyon, about boating the Colorado through this gorge, that traps us? Unbelievable splendor, to be sure. Unimaginable adrenaline surges, as we challenge our abilities against a benevolent force far greater than us, and survive to do it again. And the intoxicating yet sinister ego adventure of becoming a godlike figure to group after group, guiding them, Charon-like on a river that terrifies and bewilders the unfamiliar. Sometimes we even believe that, too. With luck and with time these intoxicants subside, however, and a deeper, more powerful relationship grows–with the Canyon and her pulsing heart, the Colorado.

It's not just Grand Canyon, of course, nor only the Colorado. There's the unholy terror of Cataract Canyon at 70,000 cfs; the enchanting spirescapes of Tower Park on the Green River; the hell of the mosquito-hatch at Sand Wash; the rattling cottonwood groves of Desolation and the San Juan; the dread of the entry move at Hell's Half Mile; the glorious tapestried labyrinths of the Yampa; the ruby sunset, exploding full moons, and the trillion-star nights above them all. It's all the River, the Canyon.

Life down here becomes more elemental, more tactile and immediate. Windstorms drive us to shelter; flash floods send us scrambling; boats roll over in the great torrents; people get skinned, bumped, occasionally broken, and sometimes even fall in love. There are hazards. But rare is the problem that is not solved quickly, soon transitioning into yet another story. It is a rugged life, sometimes edgy, often gritty, but in the end sublimely rewarding.

Boatmen, male and female, soon realize they are part of a caring and committed community, connected by their oar, their tiller handle, their paddle, to one another, grounded in the common flow. It is a connection that far outlasts the job itself.

Many of our passengers may go home with little more than pictures, stories, and sand in their ears. But some–enough–are affected deeply. Transformed. Reborn. Not every passenger, not on every trip, but enough to know that we are helping shift humanity just a tiny bit in the right direction.

But relationships with fellow guides and passengers pale compared to the one between guide and the Canyon, boatman and the Colorado. Although some new guides may boast of their prowess, it is a thin facade, quickly shattered by humility and profound respect. No seasoned guide denies who is really in charge here. It is an honor and a privilege to remain in her–the River's–bosom.

Amil knows all this.

I had been in the business for ten years when Ken Sleight took me to dinner at the Arbon Café in Green River. He said, "I want you to meet Amil Quayle. You'll like him. He's the salt of the earth." A tribal elder. A name from river lore. Ken was right. I like him. He is the salt of the earth. An instant friend that I knew I could trust, count on, look in the eye, share a story with.

Ten more years passed, and there was no denying that the River had utterly captured me. A nonprofit guide organization sprouted up–Grand Canyon River Guides– and I found myself the editor of their journal, *The Boatman's Quarterly Review*. An envelope arrived one day with a poem called "Stairways," recalling the joy and pain of being a boatman, displaying the lasting scars on the writer's soul. It was from Amil. I had lost track of him. I didn't know he was a poet. But he was, and is. His words evoked feelings I did not know I had. Every so often another poem would arrive (such as "Shawn" or "Old Boatmen Revised") and each would jar something else loose inside.

More time passed, and a darkness began to surface inside me. Turns out the power of the River can be many things. In my case it had served as a medication for nearly three decades. But like any chronically used or abused drug, in the end it was no longer enough to mask the illness. The sweet nectar of river life suddenly turned toxic and drove me from the Canyon–forever, I thought.

When next I met Amil we shared a podium at Pack Creek Ranch where the Sleights were hosting a literary event. Amil had returned from his exile in Nebraska and was teaching writing in Pocatello, devoting ever more of his life to his art–writing, and now painting. I, too, had begun to write. Amil read a few poems. I read a few stories. Afterward we drank whiskey, and Amil signed a copy of his *Pebble Creek* for me, "Even though you've taken leave from the river for a time, I'll see you on the river."

Amil saw something I didn't–that I would return. Back home I faced the growing darkness, and with much help from friends, counselors, doctors, and wizards, I came out the other side. When the sun rose again, I did return to the River, this time in health. And every so often I almost connect with Amil on the water–it might be his son, or even his grandson, both excellent boatmen. Amil and I will still meet down here. Maybe next season. He promised.

Brad Dimock
October 2007
Deer Creek Falls
Grand Canyon

"Old Boatmen"
with Clyde Ross Morgan sculpture,
Major Powell in Sockdolager, Grand Canyon
Jim Strong, Dave Mackay, Dee Holladay, Clyde Ross Morgan,
Amil Quayle, Paul Thevenin, Art Fenstermaker, Ken Sleight

Special thanks to the Quist family and crew at Moki Mac Expeditions and the Mackay family and crew at Colorado River and Trail Expeditions for always being there for me and my family and for the support and encouragement that made this book possible.

Amil Quayle

Grand Canyon

I speak now of that Grand Canyon
which lies within each of us. There
are pre-Cambrian rocks at the center,
the core, and talus from yesterday's fall;
marble and granite grown hard from the
pressure and heat of heartbreak and
passion; crumbling sandstone, layer on
layer of sediment, sentiment piled on
over a lifetime's experience. The sun
bursts on us each morning then dies
and we are in darkness, but moon shadows
tease our walls. We listen to the pulsating
rhythm of time's river lapping at our
shores. The sandy places slide, diffuse,
move closer to the sea. A billion years
of erosion is magnified, demagnified into
sixty or seventy years as we measure time.
Perhaps in a million years your shinbone
will be a fossil in another Grand Canyon,
cold in a bed of rock next to mine.

Go There

Anything you have read about the Grand Canyon is a lie
Language falters and dies before the fact
The experience is inexpressible in words
The Grand Canyon is its own language
Written across space, causality and time
See how puny these words are
Do not believe them
Go there

Second Grand Canyon expedition, circa 1872   *John Wesley Powell*

Matisse Was Obsessed with Light

*The light is so profound, it leaves nothing
but the soul of color.*
      Matisse

What if Matisse had visited the Grand Canyon
where the light can change the color of a rock
wall a dozen times in a half hour and the river
will change from deep green to chocolate brown
after a small rain up the Paria or the Little Colorado.

What if Matisse had visited Arches, or Bryce, or Zion
or Canyonlands and watched the sun come up on a
morning after a light snow. Surely he could not have
beheld that and lived. His soul would have traveled
out of itself and his brushes would have turned to
slithering snakes in his hand. His paint would have
sunk with shame into the desert sand and if he had
placed any on canvas the art Muse would have
descended from the heavens screaming, "Imposter!
Imposter!"

And yet one is saddened viewing *Lady on the Terrace,
Landscape Viewed from a Window* and *The Casbah Gate*
that Matisse didn't come to the American Southwest when
he decided to go to Morocco to "effect the necessary transition"
of going back to nature without betraying his abstract art.

Sons and Rivers

Born into the dark cradle of mechanization
they survived to find the rivers.
Peace from the engines for a time,
while modern voices said they were wrong:
irresponsible, unreliable, inefficient,
not like a smooth running motor
turning to the dictates of a time clock.
They listen to the voices and believe,
not wanting to go against other people,
being overwhelmed by industrial modes.
Who could fight it at last?
And yet they know.
They have been to the rivers,
heard the sound of water over bedrock
hollow and clear:
the low gurgle of an eddy,
the roar of Lava Falls,
the silence of flat water.
They have seen the trout break the surface.
They have thrown in a pebble.
They know and can go to a river.
They can take their sons and daughters
to a place where smooth and shiny stones
show clean through the clear glacial water,
and the color is dark green,
or where silt floats heavily
with not a visible bottom to behold.
Perhaps there will be some left then
perhaps they will go to the rivers.

Grandson and Grand Canyon

The picture of my grandson is juxtaposed against the image,
A giant laser print taken off Toroweap Point.
He is two and a half months old, warm and helpless,
Smiling out from under questioning eyes.
His father is somewhere in the canyon,
At the top of Crystal perhaps or maybe asleep in Bass Camp.
How many times in his young life did he wonder
       where I was in the canyon?
I stare at the canyon photograph
Then that of the boy.
Two magnets in the west.

Why do I peck away at this typewriter
In Nebraska?
There is nothing to keep me here.

Does the distance intensify the pleasure
Of grand created works?
The canyon looks perfect in the print.
The boy looks perfect in the print.
Is it that I am flawed and don't want them to know,
The canyon or the boy?
The mystery of the universe lies at the bottom of the canyon
And the boy.
Have I disappointed the universe?
But how could I not?
Perhaps the universe would scoff at the Grand Canyon.
Where then would I be?

But I look at the boy
And the other print,
Coin a definition for Grand,
Tell the universe it must wait.

This world has more, much more than I can bear.

Ode to Shorty Burton at Upset Rapid

Quiet cowboy man,
working for the son
of the man you started with,
you never complained
though the lines in your face
told the story.

You had children,
a small ranch to support.
Lava Falls and Crystal seemed
easy in the face of that.

Who thought you would drown
at Upset, struggling with
a knife to free yourself
from the life jacket
caught on the motor mount?

The Grand Canyon works
in mysterious ways, Shorty.
You wouldn't like it now,
thousands of people and boats
by the hundreds.

You did it right. You had it
when you were young
then left with dignity.

Those of us who remain,
salute you as we pass by here,
trying to recapture what is lost.

Old Boatmen Revised

(After consulting my good friend, Captain Myron Cook, whose inner child is alive and well.)

Old boatmen, like old cowboys,
Don't know what to do with
Themselves. They move around
Cities like feral cats. When they
Drive alongside rivers they curse
The unrunnable rapids and they
Are disappointed with the flat water.

They curse the ex-wives they
Left for the rivers. They curse
The rivers for stealing them away
From their families. They grow
Restless when they don't see a
River for a week and taxicabs
Give them claustrophobia and
Threaten them more than the
Memory of Crystal Rapid in the
Grand Canyon. Canyon sunsets
Appear when they are jaywalking
Over to the espresso for coffee.

They say the names of rapids
Over and over, afraid the oncoming
Dementia will make them
Forget. They realize their hands
Are cupped around imaginary oars
While watching Willie Nelson
Sing "Whisky River" on CMT.

Or their hands are reaching to
Give the old Mercury more cob.
"I reached to give her more cob
And there weren't none," Smuss
Allen would say when telling that
Story, and "Old fiddles play the
Sweetest music," telling that story.

He was getting older when I knew
Him on the river. Then I quit seeing
Him and I did not want to know
What happened to him or where he
Went. I saw some of the others who
Came back. Jimmy Jordan. Doc
Marston. Mack Miller. Bill Belknap.
They had been giants on the river.

Maybe Shorty Burton did it right.
Check out early in a respectable
Rapid before the pathos of old age
Competes for your soul. Wins your
Soul. Wins your mind and body.

Old boatmen know their life was
Better than most but that brings
Little comfort. He knows he is a
Driven man and always was. It
Haunts him, even when the river
Flows gently by, teasing that inner
Child that still nestles snugly there
In the restless and troubled mind.

The inner child who stood laughing
While watching the eighteen waterfalls
Coming off the rims after a flash flood
At Saddle Canyon. That inner child
Whose heart raced with excitement and
 Fear the first time he beheld Crystal Rapid.

That inner child who still lives in the old
Boatmen who have outlived their lives.
All the old boatmen I have known. And
All the old boatmen and cowboys I have
Not known. Salud. I hope your journeys
Into oblivion were, and will be, as smooth
As a perfect run through Lava Falls. As
Joyous as riding point up the trail to Abilene.

Salud. To the ones I knew, it was an honor
And a privilege. It is a gift beyond my
Expectation. It is beyond my comprehension.

It is sublime.

An Invocation

So you placed the cold steel barrel against
your brow and squeezed it off.

What did
you say to yourself at that instant? Did you
call the Grand Canyon a great whore? Did
you cry out to the Hydes and Bert and Shorty
and the Howlands that you were coming too?
Did you quietly whisper a woman's name?
Did you shake the non-trigger fist in the
air and curse some Christian God? Did you
see the faces of your children, and did you
speak their names? Did you, in reverence,
say, "Crystal," "Lava Falls," "Hermit," "Horn,"
"Upset?" Did you, at the point of impact,
see a sunrise from Nankoweep Camp?
Or was it dark like Stanton Cave?

Is it
merely a little more than nothing, a small
ring, strewn with dead amoeba from a dried
up pool in slickrock? Does the Colorado run
through it like a dancing ghost you can
approach but never touch? Are the
dam builders there, trying to stop that dance?
Is the water turbulent? Calm and peaceful?
Are the rivers runnable? Unrunnable and so
wild they grip you like a heart vice? Please
tell us, fellow river runners, fellow sojourners,
Comrades. Tell us.

A boatman falls asleep in the Grand Canyon 1969

smells the napalm and wakes the camp crying out in Saigon
telling the girl good-bye as bad as anything in the war and
coming back to a wife never loved and not his child her taking
up on the side again with the child's father going on the river
to make it easier for them not wanting to give the child up the
woman on a trip using him to father her child knowing he
would never see her or it again the whapwhapwhap of a
horizontal rotor and the crack of rifles mixed with the smell of
fuel and blood the villager limp in his arms dead the chopper
falling straight down lying in the mud pretending death for
three days until they left and the canyon walls slowly coming
together shutting out the light of the stars asleep

Stairways

The only good thing about this apartment
Is the way the wooden stairway wobbles back and forth
It feels risky and nice
I'm sure it'll collapse some day
Somebody might get hurt
I always wonder if this will be the time
Is this what old river runners do after they have long since
    given up on running rapids
Worrying about other people getting hurt
Wondering at the high cost of each epiphany
Sacrificing love for the one sublime minute in Lava Falls
Betraying family and friends for the passion of water and rock
Taking their physical needs eagerly at random when it comes
Crying lonely at the shock of Las Vegas after the trip ends
Sleeping fitfully to the sound of Phantom jets by
    Nellis Air Base
Spending the horrendous post-trip letdown day in
    The Buckskin Bar in Kanab
Listening to gloomy Ray Price singing Kristofferson songs
Returning to the warehouse with a whiskey head that feels
    like an atomic explosion
Unloading the truck of gear from the dead river trip
Wondering about this person from Cincinnati
That person from Philadelphia
Hoping to God they never see the one again
Praying to God they see the other some day
Knowing they probably never will
Loading for the next trip
Driving to Lee's Ferry
Spending a bad night
Waiting for the passengers

Sizing them up when they arrive
Going back on the water again
Nine days of agonized ecstasy
Over and over
Until it was over
Is this what old river runners do
Climb the rickety stairs of their lives
Wondering with mild amusement when
      the stairway will collapse

Brautigan Farewell 1985

Today I leave Nebraska for some trout fishing
    in the Grand Canyon.
This time I will fish from the rim.
Great silversides will come up the trail to meet me.
Grand Canyon Trout Fishing in America Shorty will be there,
    leaning against a ranger station.
The last time I fished a medium-sized trout in Lava Falls
    caught my boat alongside and over she went.
Damn near drowned everybody.
A woman from Chicago said, "Do you call this fun?"
"No, but I don't know how to do anything else."
"You don't know how to do this."
She had a point.
"It was the trout," I said.
"Trout be damned," she answered.
"I agree," said I, and commenced to fix dinner.
After we ate, the woman from Chicago took me behind a rock
    and showed me a little calfhide purse. It was smooth
    as suede and full of money.
Two days later she was casting out into Lake Michigan from
    the balcony of her condominium on Lake Shore Drive.
I was in the Fredonia warehouse cleaning 2,429 Grand
    Canyon brook trout out of the bottom of the boat.
Once out they danced on their tails all the way to
    The Buckskin Bar.

Big Montana Sky

I read it somewhere.
A rancher in Montana
sold half his ranch
to somebody on the east
coast for a garbage dump
for money to save the other half.
There was a picture of him,
watching the trucks hauling it in.
His face was blank.
The camera caught
a worried man,
sending his kids to college, perhaps,
maybe feeding ten special horses.
Knowing, probably,
that he gave up more
than just a ranch.

View south from Phantom Ranch *M. J. Colter*

The Mules at Phantom Ranch

Now they are the "old days" for us
But in the sixties we would listen to Ted Hatch
Talk about the "old days"
When his father and Rod Sanderson,
Nevilles and the others were running.

I never thought then would soon be the "old days" for us
But they are,
And hazy faces glide by
Among the problems of growing old,
Smile out from the bitterness
Residue of a retired river runner

Who does not fit in, never did,
Not in this world without a river to run.
Even the mules at Phantom Ranch
See the river every day
On their way down or up.

Sawtooth Range

A man walked into the Sawtooth Mountains
In the middle of December on snowshoes
And froze to death. It was revealed at the funeral
That he was an adopted child who had spent
The second half of his twenty years looking for
His real parents. His name was Thurgood Marsh
And he once asked me if I could guess his
Real name just by looking at him. "No," I said.
"Me either," Thurgood said, "but I never look in
The mirror without thinking about it." I have
Often wondered if he knew at the moment of his
Death. Or are there names in death?

The Death of Ed Abbey

Somewhere in a desert southwest
Edward Abbey lies,
Penelope cries in Crete,
knowing full well that Telemachus
is no longer safe.

For though Odysseus is home at last
for good, his enemies, if they knew
his place, would dance upon the grave,
poisoning first the coyote
lingering there, then shooting with spotlight
all the other eyes:

desert owl, silver fox, old man turtle,
rattle snake and kissing bug; filling
their own convoluted wish for death
by decree of death for other living forms,
as though in doing that, they somehow
die themselves without the pain
of death, and do, they get their wish.

For as each animal or plant is killed,
humans are killed to that same degree,
and though they may still walk about,
an essential ingredient has fled and
left a hidden wound, only discernable
to Muhammad, the supreme prophet,
somewhere in the Southwest Desert.

Shawn

Shawn from Poetry Writing calls.
"We have a permit to run the Selway.
It's running high. The ranger says it's
dangerous. I'll have to miss a couple
of classes. What do you think?"

What do I think?
I think I am fifty-five years old.
I think about Currey flipping five out of six boats
    on the Selway that time.
I think about finding the drowned man in Cataract.
I think about Scott drowning in flat water at the Moab Bridge.
I think about my three flips and people in the water who
    depended on me for their safety.
I think of seeing my son disappear when the tubes separated
    at Cataract and John Kingsley grabbing his arm and
    hanging on.
I think of the gut retching truth of Crystal, the Les Oldham
    truth of Warm Springs, and the Shorty Burton truth
    of Upset Rapid.
I think of Thevenin Falls on El Sumidero and Paul
    two days on that rock.
I think of every lonely night I ever spent in a sleeping bag
    by myself, listening to the sound of running water.
I think about what a person gives up for that,
    the price one pays.
Then I think about Shawn, holding the phone, waiting
    for an answer, and I say, "Hell yes, I think you
    should do it. What have you got to lose?"

My Sons, There Were Other Times

He squatted under the tree preparing the little fire, and she squatted down too, her hands smoothing water from her belly, struck forward against the warmth. The two trout he'd caught by hand, to her pleasure and girlish shrieks, lay between them on a clean cloth once part of a dress.
                    Warren Fine, *Their Family*

When we were young,
your mother and I,
before we found the world,
which was waiting for us there
in our neophyte innocence,
the terms of your conception,
we chased the trout,
its dorsal fin out of the water,
up the spillway in Sand Creek,
your mother shrieking and
laughing behind me, saying,
get it get it and I did,
the only fish we caught that day,
and the rainbow pink sides
glistening in the sunshine,
the quivering movement as
we laid it open, the eggs dropping
to my fingers' touch, taking
the bottom fins too, feeling
membrane all the way up in the throat
and the rich red blood on the grass
where it lay, cleansed, and did not
move, eyes half open, there
in the sun until a young bull moose

came by, startling us.
It was a rainbow
and we built a little fire and
cooked it there, looking at
each other in wonder at our new
discovery as we shared the fish
with our fingers, each feeding
the other and how natural it
was, without salt, or lemon,
or tartar, then we swam and
washed each other before
heading back and we knew
our lives would never be the
same but we couldn't yet know
the real joys of that day, a son,
as the other pleasures would fade
and die in the faceless reality
of a different world.

For All My Grandchildren

Grandson and Granddaughters
Am I the mystery to you
My grandfathers were to me?
Grandpa Quayle's cloud hung
Over the family like a stick,
The measuring rod of all who
Were to come after, not by his
Decree but theirs. By the
Guilt that came when his dream
Died in their laps, and though
It was more the times than the
Men and women, guilt has a way
Of missing the mark by miles.
So we the grandchildren watched
Our parents and aunts and uncles
Live in that cumulus tornado of
Ulcerative hypertension with the
Comic occasional arrogances that
Came as a carryover from the way
They had lived. I saw Grandpa Severe
Once that I remember. He had
A long gray beard and held a
Guitar, but I felt he didn't like me.
Probably he didn't know how
Excited I was to see him come in
From the sheepcamp for a day,
But that is only conjecture on my
Part, because I was only four.
He died soon after that. His sons,
My heroes, went off to war.

When they came home things
Had changed. I was eight years old
For one thing, but wars change
Everything. The world was different.
My uncles went off to Oregon to
Make saddles. I hardly ever saw
Them again. Then suddenly I
Was a father. I thought nothing
Could match that but it was only
The beginning. Now you are here.
Live your lives free. Love me if
You want, but never allow me to
Make you feel guilt. Make your own
Lives, and keep in mind that most
Of us do what we can with what we
Have been given. Forgive us if you
Can, as we have tried to forgive those
Who went before us, learning as it
Went along that every human faces
The same ultimate questions. Having
Little else to leave you, I leave you
This poem.

Digging Postholes

Dad bought a Dodge troop carrier with real bullet holes after World War II. He mounted a posthole digger on the back and went into business for himself. 10 cents a hole. I was eight years old and worked as his apprentice, learning the business from the ground up, as it were. Ernie, my older brother, drove the carrier. Dad controlled the digger manually, walking along behind. And I apprenticed. Got ready. I plotted to take over the business one day. I would keep my father on in some capacity and make my brother a foreman. They would each earn a big salary. The first thing I was going to do was buy out Ben Frei, who made Dad pay cash for the adaptation work before he let the digger leave his shop. I would call the business Amil's Post Hole Digging and Chevrolet Garage. Dad had paid for getting the digger out with a hundred dollar advance from a Camus Meadows rancher who wanted a thousand holes. He had not anticipated the rock factor, and we only had about fifty holes by the time it began to rain in late afternoon. It was forty miles of dirt road back to town, and we ran out of gas ten miles before we got there. Walking along that muddy road in the downpour, carrying a gas can, I decided I was going to make some changes when I took over.

My Father's House

Working with working people
My friend Bill the Minister said
Has made me come to realize
How often people can be knocked down
And still go on

Last summer I restored my father's house
Saw again the courage in each nail
The faith in each board
The simple hope in each plastered wall
And there were walls to be sure
And doors and more doors
And I wondered if they were added to be opened
Or closed and for whom or what against

Through all the schemes of men
To hold him down
The house still stands
The children all grew to adulthood save one
And my father in death has achieved a kind of victory

As I pulled away some walls
Tore doors off their hinges
Begged for more light into the house
It came to me
My father never took the advantage in a business deal
Allowed himself to be considered a fool
Rather than best another in a trade

I forgave him for the time I needed basketball shoes
Then I started to work on forgiving myself
While trimming the Colorado spruce
He planted when I was a boy

The Octogenarian

For Uncle Pete Quayle, a natural farmer

Now he speaks to the children
in Bonnie Hansen's day care center
the same way he spoke caringly to
a field of potatoes, warning
that they have only until fall
to rise and bloom and then die.

He never liked the harvest,
rushed through it like a non-
believing minister rushes through
a funeral, only to satisfy a requirement,
put by a little money in order to
grow a next year's crop.

The fun was in the growing,
this he knew, and in the songbird
that came with the spring, frogs
that came alive with the ditch filling,
and the pheasant making her nest.
It was a celebration of all living things.

Now as death approaches
he sees it in the round,
the endless circle of all things,
and it occurs to him over and over
that the children are eaten potatoes
and the potatoes are merely pre-children.

The songbird is in the frog and
the frog is in the pheasant.
His death will be the end of nothing.
He will rise again as a wheat shaft
or a grey sugar pea, or he will blow softly,
coming down through the canyon like a south Idaho wind.

A Memory

I remember being in Yellowstone in the Gallatin Valley the summer Dad worked up there and barking the tree the ranger coming by later scaring the hell out of us the fear of going to jail and the first inkling of an alien world and the law a rich tourist coming by and offering my parents money for one of us in earnest or in jest I cannot say but it gave me mixed emotions because I sensed we were poor and the money might have solved some of that and the mechanic who fixed our Model A charging us nothing and the folks talking about it after how he said he would nick the next rich tourist in a Cadillac and stopping along the way for the five gallon cans of gas in the culverts the tanker drivers stashed coming in with government supplies the working men taking care of each other then back in the lower valley the Model A like one of the family and how we cried when Bert Rawson handed over five twenty dollar bills and drove it away taking not only our transportation but our garden pump power source the rear end jacked up and running the v-belt directly off the tireless wheel to the pump and hearing Dad coming on the rim after a flat and no patching material and checking the lunch box for leftovers and there always were he knew and lining up the four of us like cannon balls with him on his back on the floor and shooting us off into space with his feet against our buttocks and we were happy then and Midie the one-eyed cocker spaniel and the old lame Guernsey cow the farmer sold us because he said she always had bull calves and she had twin heifers in the middle of the night and how he woke us up and led us single file out into the barn he moved from a farm to our town lot the twins both up and sucking when we got there and we were wide awake at the wonder of it and how we cried again when that same cow drowned on the end of her

stake rope trying to get a drink off the steep bank by the power
house and they pulled her out with a truck and dragged her to
the junks like an old dead tree and we were suddenly older
and something had passed and it would never come back
but it would always be there too in the middle of the night
sometimes waking suddenly it is there or seeing a small boy
with a black dog or a Guernsey cow grazing beside a river or
a Model A on a country road brings it back flooding into the
mind a sharp momentary image and the fading away and you
say to it no don't go yet there is no particular hurry is there
and it laughs at you then and hands you five twenty dollar bills
and drives away and as it rounds the corner you hear a muffled
Ahh-ooga Ahh-ooga and it is gone.

Our Mother's Garden

For Mom

Our father was a dreamer
who gave it all away,
trusting in Providence
and in men who
could not be trusted.
A hard worker who
kept no handle on the
wages he brought in.

It was our mother's
garden raised the family,
and the milk cow he
had the wisdom to keep,
even after cows were
no longer in style.

We had a few steady
milk customers, sold
raspberries, strawberries,
and that money went
in a bowl somewhere,
until things got really bad.

For years after that,
I thought it had all been wrong,
as I watched the merchant hype
that promised the golden age
and appeared to bring it on.

Now we see they were right,
the ones who made the most sense,
but not many know how to go back,
and where can one buy
a good family cow,
or get a herder for a quarter a day?

Boy and Dog on the Dam

After my mom went to sleep, I raised the bedroom window and let myself out feet first onto the damp grass. Midie was waiting beneath the window, and I said, "Shh! Quiet, Midie. Quiet, boy." He followed me around the corner of the house and along the unpainted picket fence to where the fence met the sidewalk and a big blue spruce grew. I slid in between the fence and the tree, and Midie got nervous when I disappeared. I could hear him whining and said, "Shh! Quiet, Midie. Don't wake her up." Midie got quiet, and I stood motionless for awhile looking out from the needled branches back toward the house. No lights came on, and I ran my right hand in towards the center of the tree, working it up and down. Finally it touched the cold metal, and I felt along the round pencil-shaped rod until my hand touched the cork handle. I cupped my hand over the reel and turned left, sliding out from the other side of the tree and pulling the fishing pole with me.

There was an exposed sliver of moon off my left shoulder, but it was a dark night and Midie was coal black. I could barely make out his outline in front of me. His owner was going to have him killed because he lost one eye in a hunting accident. I suppose he was afraid a cocker spaniel would miss birds with only one eye. I didn't care about that so much. I liked him the way he was, and I hate to say it, but I was almost glad it happened because I wouldn't have gotten him otherwise. He could see better than me at night.

We could hear the low, far off sound of shallow water running over lava rock, and it must have made Midie feel exactly the same way I did because he was running out in front of me like he wanted me to hurry. I followed, keeping to the tree shadows when I could. I figured old Mr. Tuck would be awake, and sure enough, there was a light in his window. He was a pretty good old man, but he was a worrier and he was always afraid some kid was going to drown. I called Midie in close, and we crossed the road before we got even with his house. I don't know why he didn't sleep at night like other people.

The sound of the moving water changed as we got closer, it sounded more real–like you would expect running water to sound. It lost the hollow sound that made a person lonesome listening to it. But sometimes you felt good listening to it and hoped your dad was near a river somewhere in France so he could hear it too. There was a feeling that came over you, and you knew a river was one of those things that a boy and a man could both understand about the same. The river was talking to you and telling you that it was all right and you might as well go to sleep. It was funny though, the river sounded different when it was cloudy or clear, and when you woke up alone in the middle of the night, you could tell what the weather was like by the sound of the river.

Me and Midie almost started running when we got close enough to see the reflection of moonlight on the rippling water. Midie was out in front and started across the canal check on the dam ahead of me. The overflow was running a lot of water down the spillway. White foam danced where it plunged into the rocks at the bottom. Midie was over the check and the overflow before I had worked my way slowly around the three-foot gate wheels that controlled the amount of water going into the canal. I started across the two-by-twelve board catwalk over the overflow, and Midie stood looking back from the other side. I could see him better now because there was some moonlight reflection off the water.

He whimpered at me as I crossed and barked once when I stepped off the end onto the dam, then he turned and ran full speed along the top of the gravel pathway. I knew he wouldn't stop until he got to the end, but then he would come back to meet me.

The only thing the dam did was divert water for the canal. It didn't even run all the way across the river. It was built in a bend of the river, so it ran right up the middle of the river, splitting it in half. The north side was like a lake, and the rest of the water running around the end of the dam and over the bedrock was what gave the river its sound. The moonlight on the south side shallow water was all shimmery, and I stopped and looked at it for a long time before I went on. Midie came back for me, whimpering like he thought something was wrong. Finally I gave in and said, "All right Midie, I'm ready to go now. I was just looking at the water." He stayed with me on up the dam and didn't make a sound when Old Nick the beaver splashed his tail as we went by. There were lots of beaver and muskrats along the dam. I just called them Old Nick for something to do.

When we got to the end, I sat down and took the Prince Albert Tobacco can from my shirt pocket. Midie started acting weird. He always did that until we caught the first fish, then he settled down. I ran my finger into the can until it touched a worm. The worm disappeared at the touch, and all I could feel was dirt. I placed the can between my knees and got my thumb down in there too until I had one caught. I started talking to him as soon as he was out. I wonder why I did that before I put him on the hook. I guess it made it easier to talk to something before you did it in. Like that Tokyo Rose that I heard Mom and Mrs. Jackson talking about. It's the same thing, only this was just a worm. Dad was in France, so he didn't have to listen to her anyway. I heard somewhere that the Americans and Germans were so close to each other in that other war that they could hear each other talking when they weren't shooting. I guess that's about the same thing, too. I couldn't see the worm, but it felt like it was on pretty good and was still wriggling when I threw him out. Fish like that.

The first one hit hard, and I figured he swallowed it deep and would probably be dead before I got the hook out and had him back in the water. Midie wouldn't eat them, so it was a waste, and I couldn't take him home 'cause that would end my fishing. It turned out the hook wasn't so deep after all, and old silversides was still in pretty good shape from the feel of him when I threw him back. We caught six or seven more just like that, and then Midie began to whine. Some dog. Didn't even think I was smart enough to know when it was time to go. Back in bed, I listened to the far-off sound of the river and wondered if my dad was anywhere near a river in France.

"My father, Tom Quayle (center), with Boy Scouts in Yellowstone in 1928 International Truck"

The Death by Drowning of My Brother Cheddy

After a child dies,
everybody dies.
There are a million little deaths
each day from that day on.

One surviving picture,
Grandma's house in the background,
on that aluminum tricycle
with one red steel wheel
Dad found somewhere.

No tall trees,
the neighborhood was young.
Glen Orgill still lived in the other house
and played his violin.

He was lucky.
He never saw a television set.

The bibs Cheddy wears are homemade,
like ones I used to wear,
thumbs under the straps,
showing them to my now dead
uncle at the reunion.

The unpaved road behind
where an old man stopped
to take the picture,
bringing it by later.

I own the house now
and the Maytag washer

where she stood
when he drowned,
washing for twelve,
the youngest only a feel
in her abdomen.

Dad in Yellowstone,
alone in that camper
he built on the pickup
and came home on weekends.

So he fell in and drowned,
the current of the irrigation
canal must have carried him away
like a piece of three-year-old cordwood

and we lay awake at night
sometimes, wondering what
it was like, how it felt to die,
sometimes jealous, wishing
it had been us, watching our
parents grieve, learning ourselves
how to grieve, while trying
not to forget something
fine, that came a day and
left.
A brother.
A picture.
A tricycle.
Grandma's house.

Riding Icebergs on the Snake River

In the springtime
we rode the icebergs on Henry's Fork.
Billie Barrot had a long pole.
My brother Ernie had an axe.
I was little and had nothing.
They liked it that way;
it made them responsible.
They knew if I drowned
they'd catch it at home for days.
We'd cut one off and jump aboard,
but one time it split.
Billie and the pole
going one way,
my brother and I the other,
out in the current
toward the dam.
Billie poled ashore,
ran downstream,
threw the pole like a javelin.
It was in the water
three feet from the berg.
My brother lay on his stomach,
held on to my feet
while I sat holding
the opposite side of the berg,
reached out his toe,
dragged it back.
Water over the dam
was deafening.

My brother pushed
with the pole, slipped off
and was swept under the berg
as it struck the dam,
which was an oblique angle
across the river.
The iceberg shook and heaved
against the concrete.
My brother appeared
and clutched at the berg
as it began to slide
against the dam,
taking us toward the shore.
After Billie pulled him out,
my brother could walk
but couldn't speak.
As we hurried home,
Billie expounded
on the principle of the iceberg,
displacement, friction,
and other important matters,
which I have long since forgotten.

The Beet Dump

For my dad, who hauled beets in a 1928 International Truck

There is no date on the picture
and no names.
There are nine men,
two four-horse hitches and a team,
three wagons full of sugar beets.
They are on the high part
of a trestle over a railroad car
thirty feet in the air.
A boy is standing below the structure
leaning against an upright.
One man is wearing a tie, vest and felt hat.
The others wear bib overalls.
They are looking towards the camera.
Where was the picture taken?
What year?
How many wagons
dumped their beets that day?
When was the trestle built?
Where did the lumber come from?
How many of those men died in the war?
What was really lost
when the teams
were sold for dogmeat
and the men
surrendered themselves
to machines?

A Good Portion of My Tongue Lies Buried with the Lincoln School

As soon as the weather cleared icy gusts drove through every chink and cranny, leaving white frost behind; people's breath hung frozen in the air the moment it was out of the mouth; if one touched iron, a piece of skin would be torn away.
                        O. E. Rolvaag, *Giants in the Earth*

Grades one through four,
and I got Miss Welker twice,
twice I say,
in first and second grade,
I, who was born under the Ram,
first sign of the zodiac
into which the sun enters March 21st,
spent two years of winter in the clutches
of the quintessential old-maid
school teacher and principal
who had the added burden
of caring for her aged mother,

who, when my fourth grade brother
sluffed school because she slapped
him at recess, brought him next
morning in front
of the second grade class and asked
him why he left.
Because you hit me he said,
wincing as she grabbed him and shook.
I didn't hit you did I?
Yes.
I didn't hit you did I?
Yes.

I was impressed and looked around the
class with pride.
I didn't hit you (shaking harder) did I?
No.

I guess it had to end.

And when I stood with the full
face of my tongue stuck to the steel gatepost
when the bell rang, all the boys and girls
lined up holding hands,
Miss Welker like a drill sergeant,
looked over her shoulder and saw me there,
kind of leaning over,
waiting for something to happen,
came running out,
grabbed me around the waist,
and yanked me away
and I saw that blue meat
still on the post
and didn't speak for weeks.
Or years.

They razed that school,
dozed it into the basement,
fence and all;
somebody was going to build
a market, but they never did.

The lot lies empty now,
and the windows on Miss Welker's house
are boarded shut.
I drive by every summer
when the weather is sunny and warm,
searching for my tongue,
silent against the post,
a gate that couldn't open.

Lincoln Schoolhouse　　　　　　　　　　　　*St. Anthony, Idaho*

Music Appreciation and President John F. Kennedy

A runner broke the news;
He burst through the door
Into 118 Freedom Hall.
"They killed Kennedy!"

Professor Highnote rose to the occasion
She said it was terrible
But it shouldn't interfere
With our ability to appreciate music.

Then she played something by Bach.

Poetry as Metaphor

Ask what unifies the context?
What is the central theme?
Does everything revolve around the main point?
I can still hear Miss Ames,
telling us how it should be.
She was proper, prissy,
and virginal.
Lasted until she was thirty-nine,
loved poetry with a rhyme,
thought students were sublime;
until he hit town.
Suddenly she came around,
came to school with her hair let down,
danced on her desk,
picked a blue guitar.
She told us poetry was what you feel
not what you see on the page.
The meaning is inside (she said).
The words need no referents or antecedents
if they touch the right spot.
Poetry is a way of seeing.
Poetry is a way of being.
Read the poem whole,
don't try to break it down.
Trust your own instincts.
Then he left town
as quietly as he came,
and she arrived at school
with her hair in a bun,
smashed the blue guitar on a verb,
and we diagrammed sentences
for the rest of that year.

A Short History of World War II for the Oldest of Five Brothers

For Ernie

You remember the ranger in Yellowstone, looking in green more like Uncle Bart in the army than Pete, Blaine, Jerry, or Bill in the Navy or Duffin in the Marines. How he came after us when we barked the tree. Then coming home in the Model A to Dad's air promise of prosperous farm work in the valley. Living from the garden and the lame cow until she drowned on the tether rope and watching the farmers grow rich on Hitler prices, Dad ashamed not being in the war and giving up his land in 1934. His driving the sugar factory worker's truck, sticking it in a snow bank, the pileup of cars behind, the young soldier with a three-day pass killed. Going with him in the snow plow after a midnight blizzard. The box of Hershey's candy Pete sent from Moffett Field. The move to Salt Lake, Dad driving cab, living next to that place with huge tanks, the mean owner chasing us. Running, running. Tanks everywhere. Lost. Then downtown lost. Kind policeman giving us gum. The barbers giving us gum. Back to Idaho for more air. The radio saying it was over. People dancing in the street. Bart, Bill, Jerry, Duffin, Blaine and Pete home. You nine and could already drive a truck.

Across the Mountains with Brother Henry the Trucker

Brother Henry the trucker calls. He is dumping barley
In Pocatello. I drive to the elevator. We eat breakfast
At JB's waiting for the first truck to unload. I overload
On the buffet and Henry orders a waffle but the grille
Is cold and it is late coming so he has to gulp it down
Because we can see the first rig pulling out. The barley
Dust is dessert, rising like Montana from the grates
Below. Henry tells me the farmer put poor barley on
The bottom, trying to get a better ticket although the
Test probes reach all the way down through the load.

The fog has lifted and we close the hoppers and head
South, stopping at the weigh station in Inkom. I think
Of 1970 when we are heading south to Mexico in a
Truck half this size and pulling a 30-foot tandem trailer.
Nervous Mack Miller keeping track of the miles and
Gasoline used for Jack and Betty Ann Currey, who
Are taking us on another fun and wild adventure to
Mexico.

Henry just back from Vietnam and me still trying to
Big-brother him after all he has done and seen. How
The high truck van starts dragging on the underpasses
On the freeway into Mexico City, and we have to let
Half the air out of the tires to get through. A mile of
Cars behind us, the drivers all honking in a rage and
A foot-long hole in the top back of the van when we
Finally run out of low bridges.

Then coming to the wide river in Chiapas and the
Ferry crossing and we are the first rig on and the
Ferry leans hard to the downstream side and we think
It will surely go over. The excited Mexican attendant
Frantically waves for more cars to come onto the
Upstream side and it comes down a little. The truck is
Top-heavy with river gear and we gaze down into that
Green riley water, but we make it across, pull off,
And go on.

The agriculture and aduana stops and the little red
English-made Ford that comes after us after we run an
Ag stop. Four federales lean out the windows, all blowing
Little athletic whistles. We pay them off and go on.
The crazy flight into Trace Nationes in the old bomber
With a cockpit full of comic books and the swash
Buckling pilot who wears a WW II leather flight jacket and
Cap, a red scarf, and carries a Colt .45 on his hip. How
We drop down out of the clouds and there is a mountain
Higher than the airplane a thousand feet off the right
Wingtip. The pilot looks over at Henry in the copilot
Seat and winks.

The other four of us sitting in the cabin without seat
Belts on top of a six-hundred pound neoprene pontoon
Over the bomb bay next to a sign that reads: Maximum
Weight, 500 pounds. The wingtips cut sugar cane on
Both sides as we come in. A hundred townsmen show
To help us unload. They bring eggs and live chickens
To send back to Tuxtla with the airplane. Buck Boren
Negotiates wages in his limited Spanish for them to
Help carry the gear a half-mile to the river and the
Plantation owner is mad because he has been paying
Them about 25 cents a day.

The college group from Indiana with all the girls who
Need tans and Bob Quist stumbling out of his tent at
The crack of noon, falling headfirst into the river to
Wake up while everyone cheers.

We find long vines hanging from the tall trees in the
Jungle and Henry swings out over camp yelling, "Me
Tarzan, you Jane." The howler monkeys get into the
Noise and let out their own screams that pierce the soul.

Natives come along in hollowed out logs, cayucos,
With recently shot rodents they call tepesquintles
To sell us for dutch oven cooking for evening. They
Are delicious.

Then through the awesome gorge with shear rock
Walls all covered with jungle-green. Down the rapids,
The boats bumping each other as we go, the college
Girls yelling with delight and glee.

Mack meeting us at the end. The Mexican waiter
Calling him a "muy nervio amigo" as he waits for the
Café to open so he can get coffee at six a.m.
Heading back to the states and the difficulty crossing
Into Texas. We finally convince them we are legit
Tour people but it costs a hundred dollars to get
Out of Mexico.

Then my move to Green River and Henry back to
Idaho and me to Nebraska and all the life-happens
Episodes and twenty years have come and gone.
We turn off the interstate at the McCammon exit,
Head for Soda Springs to load fertilizer at Simplot of
Idaho Mine. Green slime oozes out a 6-inch pipe into
An open ditch. We load and head back to Pocatello.

Henry drops me at Forde Johnson's truck stop, loans
Me a hundred dollars, and I tell him to have fun in
Portland. I come back to my little trailer and read for
Tomorrow's class and wish I was headed for Portland
Instead, with my brother, Henry, the rock.

*Lyman Carlos Severe, his wife, Myrtle, and daughter,
Lillian, at sheepcamp trailer*

Grandpa Died in a Sheepcamp

I remember seeing him once,
Guitar in hand,
Long gray beard.
Leaning back on his chair
Against the kitchen wall.
I remember
Thinking he probably
Didn't like me.
His time in town
Was limited,
Had to be rationed
To his wife and twelve children.
He died at sixty-two with diabetes,
Jerry, his fourteen-year-old son
With him, who walked to town afterwards.
I have one small picture of him,
Sitting on the tongue of the camp,
His shepherd dog by his side.
Sometimes I see his brand
Cut in a quaking aspen tree
In the Shotgun Valley.
It is like an abbreviated poem
Which I proceed to write
In my own imagination.
An ode to that mysterious man
I wish I could have known.

Silence and the Coming of Spring

For Grandpa Severe

I look at my Grandfather's picture
Worncare lines of thirteen children
Written across the face under the
Long curly beard full through the
Lambing breeding and weaning of
Two thousand days and the lonely
Coyote thousand nights howling in
The sheepcamp waking to the hurt
Dreaming of a first dead wife and
The second home with the burden
Of man's desire taken the same year
I was born it is me I see in that face
As it arrives near the slaughterhouse
Past fifty with nothing but good
Memories of love and youth to
Embitter against the growing cold
Of the Idaho wind and what if I do
Not die well like him how then big
Sky stockman up there somewhere
But die I will if not well then badly
As the eagle dies after losing its
Talons to a manset trap taliped to
The agonies of some seemingly infinite
Diabolical design

100 Teams

Grandfather owned a hundred teams
before the Crash of '29.
An old man in town told me
he was giving them away
to anyone who would promise them feed
in 1934.
I was born in 1938.
I played in the barn that once housed the horses
when I was twelve years old.
My uncle took me there
with my brother and six cousins,
while he watched in dead silence.
The owners did not live there,
the brick house was abandoned,
the barn full of pigeons.
Twenty-five years later
the barn caved in and the house was razed.
Last year the trees were dozed
to make way for a pivot system,
the last death knell to sub-irrigation
Grandfather helped to establish.
I do not apologize for him
though he owned a hundred teams,
but it would have been nice
if my father had owned one
or perhaps two.
And wouldn't it be fine
if we still farmed with horses
and people didn't live in cities
unless it was their choice.

The Tallest Stone in the Cemetery

The tallest stone in the
Cemetery:
White marble,
Round ball on top,
Standing near the entrance.

I didn't know him,
My great-grandfather.
But I always wondered,
As a kid will do,
How many pairs of shoes
Went into that cold marble stone.

Saddle Musings

I keep my saddle next to the word processor for inspiration, figuring the Muse will surely come riding in on a horse. She would never ever come driving a Mercedes or even a middle class Ford; not a pickup truck; oh, maybe a seven window Chevy circa 1950, but never a new one, not my Muse. When she comes it will be on a white Arabian and her hair will fly out behind, mingling with the horse's flaxen tail. She will ride a Severe Brothers saddle and her horse's name will be Aziza. My Muse.

"Uncles Duff & Bill Severe: World Famous Saddlemakers"

"Running a Rapid," R. A. Muller engraving for J. W. Powell's second expedition, circa 1873

A Woman

I still have those fifteen shinysmooth
river rocks, the ones you gave me
for each year's difference in our age
on the Middlefork of the Salmon that
summer. How old were you then? Twelve?
Thirteen? The hermit, Bill, calling you a
nice lad and how you beat your brother
in all the games. Butch haircut and the
older woman who followed you around.

Who guessed then the woman you
would become? Perhaps your father,
who, when you were sixteen, wouldn't
let you out of his sight. Invited me into
the tent where he could watch us both.

Later you were a woman in Mexico
but I still felt those fifteen rocks
hard in my pocket like crucifixes.
Like hardened Hester scarlet letters from
our mutual Mormon background.
Together on the boat in darkness.
Like an overzealous idiot, I sent you
back to your tent without a touch.

When the Sun Went Backward in the Sky

*So the sun returned ten degrees,
by which degrees it was gone down.*
                              Isaiah 38:8, *King James Bible*

We were killing brush
in the north end of the county
along the dry farm roads
just below timberline,
with 245T, watered down dioxin,
diesel added to make it stick,
Agent Orange, though the code
name from Vietnam had not yet
been invented, nor had Vietnam–
my partners in crime, Alex from
War II, and Bill from Korea.

It was one of those Rocky Mountain
summer days in Fremont County,
crisp thin air and sun that didn't burn
the skin but played across the sky,
easy and slow, and how you could swear
it hadn't moved for maybe two hours
because you wanted to stop and lunch
in some particular place, usually a cold
stream coming down a canyon–a slight feel of
fall–it was mid-August–and already some
of the potato vines had begun to wilt,
and you were so used to the smell of
what came out the nozzles that it bothered
you no longer–it was a job and jobs were
scarce as millionaires in Fremont County.

And finally it reached the apex of your
sensibility and you stopped where you
agreed to meet Bill and Alex and waited–
falling asleep in the grass next to the truck,
but they didn't come and when you woke
the sun had retreated in the sky and it was
mid-morning and cooler and you wished you
had a watch and the world had gone strange.

They never came and you wondered, was
sure this was the right place, but you ate your
peanut butter and jellies and the devil's food,
then the cake with the thermos coffee and drove
over to Bitch Creek to refill the tank and when
you asked the fisherman for the time he said it
was half past eleven and you looked again at
the sun as you breathed in the dioxin fumes and
it was further east than it had been when you
stopped and you told yourself it was something
to do with last night's party, but it was the
Isaiah high sun, there in the Idaho sky,
having fun.

The Wood Carver

The wood carver sits in the shade
of a wooden granary needing paint
and carves a mahogany statue
of Eve tempting Adam with an apple.

Inside the house, Angeline cans tomatoes
on the Warm Morning wood cook stove,
throws in an ivory inlaid wood candlestick,
listens to the old varnish crackle in the flames.

In Kansas City, her only daughter takes money
from a man in a small room, and her
only son, twelve years dead, lies buried
in the garden to the west of the house, under strawberries.

They never pick the berries,
the robins get them all,
pluck them out like so many bloodshot eyes,
and there are bird droppings on the carved alabaster stone.

The wood carver comes in at exactly twelve,
eats the silent meat, potatoes and corn
served up for him on the single plate,
atop the intricately carved, ivory inlaid wood table

he created the first year they were married.
No words pass between them. She continues
to peel the steaming tomatoes, dropping each one in cold water
and he notices the candlestick is missing but says nothing.

He finishes and leaves the empty plate, silverware and glass,
quits the house, walks to the outside pump,
drinks from his cupped hand, fills a water bag,
catches and saddles the pony, rides slowly to the south pasture.

In summer there are always musk thistle.
The little horse recognizes them, stops without command,
and the wood carver reaches down with a shovel,
flipping them out and cutting off the liquid-filled roots.

The curious cattle come to check him out,
their dumb, drooped head stares please him,
and some day, he thinks, he'll carve a full-sized cow and calf,
or maybe a bull, if he can find a large enough piece of wood.

Angeline finishes the two dozen quarts of tomatoes,
takes the skins to the henhouse,
returns to the house by way of the garden,
where she pulls a few weeds by the strawberries.

She can hear the hens squabbling over their prize.
"What could my life have been," she starts to say,
but puts it aside, digs potatoes for supper.
The wood carver will be hungry at six, exactly.

Alex

In the fifties
working for the Fremont County Weed Control
in St. Anthony, Idaho,
we used brush killer,
245T
Agent Orange, though we didn't know it then.

I worked with Alex,
the veteran.
Seven years with the Weed Control
and five in World War II.

He was patient with me,
a high school kid,
but not careful with chemicals.
He splashed himself regularly.

I moved on and so did Alex.
He got a good government job
driving checkpoint at the AEC,
Atomic Energy Commission,
in the Idaho desert
before it became the INEL,
Idaho Nuclear Engineering Laboratories.

No matter. Alex has cancer.
Leukemia.
I saw him last summer
but didn't ask,
was it Agent Orange
or radiation?
or five years of war?
lacking two days,
as he told me once,
when in my youth,
I had mentioned something about glory and victory
or other such nonsense.

He was kind and patient,
brought some *Stars and Stripes* to work,
full of pictures of the concentration camps
and I was silenced.
He did his work without question,
raised his family,
watched his wife die of cancer,
and hasn't much longer now.

And people say
over and over,
I hope they find a cure for it,
while lobbying for more projects at INEL.

Cowboy Poet

There's something strange
it seems to me,
'bout a man so fat
he kin scarcely see
his boots;
talkin 'bout wranglin cows,
and wrestlin bulls.
Hell he couldn't touch his toes
on a ten dollar bet or free.

Looks like a man
never stayed in a shack,
or ate beans without meat,
or carried a deer on his back.

No sirree,
he don't look like no cowpoke to me.
But what do I know,
I hail from a town
near the Liberty Bowl.

I never roped a dogie,
or heard one bawl.
Hell I ain't done nothin at all.
That's why I'm so fat
I just have a ball,
watchin television.

I don't run a mile to feed no horse
or ride the whole night through–
he looks like fifteen feet,
more or less would do.

Now I ain't saying he's a liar,
course I ain't,
I'm just sayin he ain't tellin the whole truth,
and looks like he'd just faint,
if he walked to the barroom,
which is, no doubt,
where most of his cowboyin is done!
all in fun, all in fun.

"Amil & Sister"

Write a Poem about Me

"Leaving Cheyenne bound for Albuquerque,"
The old man said, climbing into my truck.
Oncoming headlights burned the eyes.
Wipers splashed rainwater from the windshield.
We rode to Trinidad in silence.
In the coffee shop he paid with a fifty dollar bill.
"Write a poem about me sometime," he said.
Here it is.

Ernie Quayle with ponies

Sister Horse

Sister horse is in foal
She looks so Mona Lisa wise
Standing in the all-knowing pasture
Swishing her tail to Beethoven's Fifth
Under the great cottonwood tree

Outcross hybrid vigor pasture bred
Naturally selected to survive in North Dakota
Her blood will mix with ancient blood
Drawn from horses by Mongols for pudding
War spilled by Seljuk Turks and Attila the Hun

The foal will bring in April
Gliding down through Nebraska winter
Like a golden chariot from Hungary
Home of stallion's forebears
Foaled in the blood of Ghengis Khan

Her foal will be the daughter or son of Taltos
Bay in Nebraska from the Bitterroot Mountains
From the resurrected remnants of the army remount
From the regal ravages of Hungarian history
Caught in the crossfire of Russia and Germany

Her foal will be the foal of the ages
The horse that carries the legions
Through the dark corridor of human existence
Into the subdued light and revelations of the moon
Into the blinding light of truth which is the sun

Her foal will fly on Pegasus wings
They will climb on its back and ride into paradise
They will discover on it the ultimate answer
They will unfold on it the mystery of the universe
They will call its name Alastor

The Sleeping Coyote

Silent on the golden stallion
I ride to the edge of a small canyon
All green with native prairie grass.
My horse stops abruptly at the edge,
His ears turned forward.

At the bottom I see a great coyote
Stretched out sleeping in the sun.
The yellow stud stands silent,
Hypnotized by the wild dog.

I am due at the house for dinner
But cannot bring myself to stir
Or cry out to the sublime canine
I am supposed to hate and kill.

Finally he lifts his head,
Licks himself about a hundred times,
Puts his head down.
Sleeps.
The breeze is blowing our way.

I reign my horse silently away,
Knowing the day has been a gift,
One of those rare moments
When all pettiness is expiated.

Riding back the horse paces himself,
In no particular hurry for grain.

To the Bobcats I Knew in 1977

You were the symbol of my last hope
when I found you there, two kits
in the old abandoned barn on the far
end of the ranch. I saw you from time
to time throughout the summer but
never told anyone, knowing they would
be there with dogs to hunt you down.
In the fall, I saw you half grown with
your mother, and how you climbed the
tree at my approach. I did not stop
though I wanted to say hello or goodbye.
Neither you nor me, it seems, were
given the right to spend our
lives on that place. But somehow I
believe you survived, and I see
you walking free, being what bobcats
are and doing the things they do, and
I try not to think of the greyhounds
and the men with rifles and pickup trucks.

The Coal Trains

Black mile-long serpents
with ominous deep death-sounding horns
roll across Nebraska in a race with Dante
for purgatory, strip mines on one end,
coal-fired generating plants on the other.
Thistles and smoke where wild grasses
and clean air once prevailed, connected
by cold steel rails, smell of creosote
and diesel, a thousand small, once
pastoral towns that vibrate and rattle
awake ten to twenty times a day, as
the dark coal dust cortege passes through.

Full cars going south pass empty cars going
north, burning energy to burn energy to
burn energy for the burning of energy's sake.
A utility company's dream and a social nightmare,
created by senators and congressmen
as unaware as the people in the towns who have
bought the notion that the quality of their lives
is insignificant compared to the magnificence
of a new Chevrolet four-by-four pickup truck,
proving, by god, they are worthy people at last.

Leaves from the Hackberry Tree

Last night it froze
today it snowed leaves
covered the house roof
patio
lawn
rabbit pens
filled the yellow wheelbarrow

sounded like corn flakes
walking through them.

I found the green plastic rake
orange snow shovel
brown plastic bag with white plastic insert
to hold it upright

created three compost piles
which will settle down
to almost nothing by spring.

It will look like black dirt
when I work it back into the soil

as I would prefer to look
when they work me back
into the soil into that green green
mystery from which I sprang

when my mother made fresh
vegetable soup from the garden
she lived in during those languid long pregnant
mountain days in southern Idaho

working the spent apple tree
leaves into the soil in the fall
and later watching the wild yellow
rose bushes die on the canal bank

after I sprayed them with 2-4D
in my youthful ignorance imagining
I was ridding her of a useless pest.

Each hackberry leaf is a
yellow rose petal as I dump
it in the pile though none
have been touched by chemicals

and I think of her with each dump
and how she forgave me
though the yellow roses
said goodbye.

Walking with Alvin

I see him on the road,
head forward,
shoulders slumped;
it is early morning,
just light.
All the land,
both sides of the road,
is his.
His life.
His universe.
He doesn't want to leave it,
can't see himself apart.
Paradise doesn't interest him
without it.
He walks past the corner,
steady and methodical,
the way he has lived,
each movement accomplishing its task,
nothing wasted.

I call my dogs,
go out to meet him.
He tells me it's fine,
he doesn't need to be alone.
He is moving faster than I thought.
That has fooled me before.
I hurry to keep up,
find myself breathing rapidly.
He has had two heart attacks,
walks for the aerobic,
after and before

a full day's work.
He tells me about his rapid pulse
as though he can't believe it,
thinking it unjust
because he has worked so hard.
I agree,
though I do not say it,
it is unjust.
Alvin is going to die,
leave all this good land.
Will the next man love it
and nurture it
the way he has?

At 50

I stargaze at the flaming fall trees,
casting yellow, purple and bronze
on the turquoise water.
Is it me I see, falling, floating, foundering,
a cherry red leaf,
fighting for a last offering of sun,
then giving in, absorbing the hydrogen and oxygen,
yielding then inviting it in?

At what point is the leaf not a leaf?
When it changes color?
When it falls from the tree?
When it sinks in the water?
After the lake is gone and it solidifies?

I will not wait for the leaf to sink,
that could take days and I haven't the time.
I stay until the sun burns out of the western sky.
The trees seem to be laughing at me now.
There are hundreds of leaves left,
black on the trees
against the deep blueblack of the moon sky.

The stars laugh, too.
"Foolish man," they say. "What do the stars know?" I ask back.
 "Nothing perhaps. Is being fifty so bad?"
"How can you ask that,
you who are billions of years old?"
"Would you change places with us?"
"Maybe," I say.
"Then you are more foolish than we thought."

A breeze comes up and more leaves fall.
I reach into the water from my rowboat,
scoop up a wet leaf.
"I'll take you home, dry you out,
put you in a book. You could last for years."
The breeze quickens, more leaves fall.
I pull the oars for awhile longer,
then feel the bow slide into the soft shore mud.

Three Loaves

It is difficult to write poetry
while listening to Beethoven
and smelling sourdough bread
baking in a woodstove oven.
Who needs it?
Who needs to write now?
Now when it feels good
there is nothing to say,
no reason to say it.
I feel so fine,
I imagine myself in heaven.
A woman has her head on my shoulder.
The dogs are asleep by the stove.
The woodbox is full.
Homemade pint jars
of peach jam line the heaven cupboard.
The cat is out for the night
playing with barn rats.
God is away on business,
something about somebody
misrepresenting his son.
Michael is playing pinochle with Lucifer.
The apostle Paul is with a woman.
Three loaves of whole wheat bread
bake in the woodstove oven.
Heaven is quiet
except for the faint sound
of a string symphony
playing Bach.

In the morning the multitudes will come
and I will divide the loaves.
All people will get the same
and everyone will have enough.

The Surprise Snow

Winter wheat cries for it
and perhaps it hears
though to count on it is folly
as She has proved so many times.

This time it comes
in giant wet flakes
painting the trees with cotton
and doesn't stop for twenty hours.

A woodpecker with a red V
on the back of his neck appears,
hugging the underside of the
big branch on the hackberry tree.

They come
when the ground is white below
and they contrast in color
with the creamy background.

It hangs upside down for two hours
filling itself with what?
Something I cannot see
though I watch the action spellbound.

The temperature reaches 32°,
milk falls from the trees,
another woodpecker appears
and the wheat drinks voraciously.

A Walk in the February Snow

My life is only the earth risen up
a little way into the light, among the leaves
          Wendell Berry, "The Morning's News"

When it starts we are disappointed,
believing we long for spring though
the fields are dry and thirsty, farmers
looking to the sky for easy answers.

It comes slow and easy in large flakes
that glide down slantwise like goose down
and the longer it falls, the more right
the world becomes until we can stand

it no longer. We become as children,
go out in it and walk to the edge of town
in silence as it circles around us
until it purges us of the day's little horrors,

the realities of what we have done to this
earth, the injustices we perform in the name
of business acumen, the shoddiness of work
poorly done and the general avarice and

fear on every doorstep. The snow cleanses and
forgives it all, takes us up into it as it covers
our heads and shoulders, absorbing all sound
save that of an internal song, a hymn of joy. A peace.

Tater, the Invincible Dachshund

Crossing the veil
is a way of life for Tater,
the invincible dachshund,
whose little
sister succumbed
to the coyotes
or some other
Sandhills force
the third day after arrival.
She was in heat and perhaps
that brought them in, but
maybe it was a badger
or a washout hole.
She never came back,
but Tater did.

A few days later Mary heard
Tater and looked up from
her planting to see a big dog
coyote carrying him over the
hill. She screamed, "Let go of
my dog, you dog!" The coyote
let go and the teeth marks
that had punctured the skin
healed in a few weeks.

She ran over his head
with the Datsun pickup.
His eyes popped out like two
little black cherries on his cheeks,
and he did not move. She rushed
him thirteen miles to the Burwell
vet. They got him going with
artificial respiration,
but for years he had seizures
and could not swim, rolling
over sideways in the water.
He would leap to sit on a chair
and miss it completely.

After the ranch rejected us, we
moved to a mobile home outside
Lincoln, Nebraska. I turned
Tater out to play, and two shepherds
got him. He had ninety-eight stitches
and only two-thirds of his left ear.

Mary and I divorced, and she
took the four dogs and the parrot
to live in Arizona. Her friend's
shepherds got him again, and he was
in doggie intensive care for awhile.

That was the last I heard until
today. A mutual friend called to
say that Mary and Jim had been
in Mexico with Tater. A Gringo-
hater shot Jim in both legs then
stole their pickup with Tater inside.
Jim is doing fine, the bullets missing
bone both times,

and when they found the pickup it
had been rolled two times, and
Tater was still in the cab, alive
but hungry.

Two Spring Rains

A couple walks by
under a red yellow gray white umbrella.
The window is open,
all students write except three:
one reads a newspaper,
another a book,
and one looks out the window,
like me,
at the building downtown
with all those flags.

The English Department should emulate that,
each professor with a little banner,
flying high over Andrews Hall:
symbol as proof of accomplishment,
area of discipline,
political philosophy.
Pennants indicating specialty,
don't tread on me isolationist lone stars
unfurled in the Great Plains wind.

Last week it rained hard
after an extended dry time,
the roof leaked through the cracked tar.
Eldon Slangle's office got drenched,
the lifetime collection of books,
indoor flags,
Moby Dick and the albatross of higher education.

As they mopped it up,
I saw on a table outside his office,
the little sculpture of three whales
swimming suspended in the air,
next to a waterlogged Bible
and some saturated short stories.

It was no longer a concern
that he had failed my exam;
that seemed far away,
like Melville and Hawthorne,
Camus dying in that car wreck,
Emily sitting alone in her room,
talking to herself with a pencil.

Now the rain comes in sheets,
the umbrella is gone,
the flags no longer visible.
The students put down their pens,
look out the window at the water,
a gift, a revelation, a beginning, a possibility.

After Twelve Years in Nebraska

I do not belong here
on this prairie,
in this mobile home
planted on cinder blocks.

I am a river runner,
a westerner,
a cowhand emeritus
from the Rocky Mountains.

And yet I stay,
not knowing why,
taking things as they come
without much question.

When I go back west
it will be sublime.
I will be old and young,
like the Tetons.

A Man Can't Hide

A man can't hide on the prairie Webb said
That's why he started wearing guns
He built a circle around himself with a Colt .45
But even then he was dead meat without a horse
My greatgreatgrandmother crossed the Plains pushing a handcart
Indian women walked behind their men who rode horses
A man can't hide but perhaps he should

Defining the Loss

How strange it is
To sit on this lot,
A hundred feet long by a hundred wide
In the middle of Nebraska
Surrounded by a chain link fence.

I have become
The divided,
Disillusioned,
Alienated
Man,
Of which
Wendell Berry speaks.

I am a product
Of the growth economy,
The military industrial complex.
I eat Wheat Chex for breakfast out of a box,
California lettuce for lunch,
Texas boxed beef for dinner.

I hear the coal trains
Every day,
On their way to Georgia
With Montana coal.
The house vibrates
And the whistles
Wake me at night.

And yet I stay,
not knowing why,

Every evening at ten
I watch the national news
And believe.

I am a man
In modern American society.

At Night in the Trailer

The loneliness and sublimity
of the universe
is contained in this trailer tonight.
The yowling Siamese
next to my chair
is the Creator.
He jumps in my lap,
contented for the moment,
purring away his fear
to the rhythm of my heartbeat.
The blue heeler dog is asleep by the couch.
I can hear the crickets
and the mourning doves
through the window screens.
Everything seems close.
I concentrate on sound
and hear far off the shifting
down of trucks on the interstate
and train whistles
blowing at crossings in a hundred
Midwest towns, hauling coal
from Montana to Georgia, cutting
through the nation like a black
burning scourge, arrogant
and loud. My mind turns away,
pushes it out, comes back to the cat,
the bird, dog and cricket,
and I sleep, waking now to the sound
of a helicopter, flying low,
probably from the base in Omaha.

The Simple Joy of Finding a Twelve-Foot Tall Sunflower Growing in My Front Yard from a Seed of Unknown Origin after Returning from a Summer in the Mountains

One would not think a sunflower on the prairie would be a pleasant thing to come home to after three months in the pines and firs of western slopes

but it is.

It looks like a mutant of some kind.

It has seven flower heads.

Perhaps it grew from what I threw out when I cleaned the parrot cage in the spring.

The parrot flew to Arizona looking for a tropical forest.

There are volunteer squashes and tomatoes here but the grasshoppers have taken their toll.

Is there a reason for grasshoppers?

Surely it must not be to keep the chemical companies alive.

Fish bait maybe.

Cranes eat fishes and are protected.

A fisherman in Idaho complained to me about that. "They aren't protected from me whenever I can get at 'em," he said.

I wonder how sunflowers and cranes relate.

Or the osprey with a two-foot high nest on the railroad bridge
west of St. Anthony, Idaho.

Every morning for five days I watched her from my camp
dive for fish in the Snake River and feed them to her babies.

Did my horse notice, grazing in her hobbles beside
the shallow water flowing noisily over bedrock lava?

Her ears kept turning to the sounds I could not hear,
but I saw no change in the eyes.

I knew a trainer once who could.

He could see an attitude change in the eyes of a horse.
"There it is," he would say and the horse would submit.

I wonder why the large flower on the plant avoids the sun.
It faces north towards my house.

Perhaps it is a mutant.

The Milford Times

The grown man stands proudly
Holding up a dead boa constrictor,
Eight feet long, shot between the eyes
Outside Milford, Nebraska.
No one seems to know
Where the snake came from.
Next to that feature
Is a small article about
The single woman school teacher
Who seduced a senior boy
And had to leave town in disgrace.
She was twenty-two.
Ruby Fuller displayed her doll
Collection at the senior citizen
Hall where punch and cookies
Were served. Errol Talbot was
Caught stealing gasoline from
Billy Davidson's farm tank. Julie
Lytle abandoned her baby in
A ditch, and some pheasant
Hunters found it, alive and well.
Old John Peter died of cancer.
Sylvia Newsome had a new baby
Girl. Her husband, George, is
Stationed in Germany. The picnic
In the square went about like it
Was planned. Thanks to everyone
Who came.

Empyrean, Nebraska

We have given ourselves no good
reason not to see in these desolate
places the future of the whole country.
             Wendell Berry

The family stays on
opening a steak house
called *The Dissolution*
in the building where
Ed Horky sold hardware.
The buildings on both
sides are empty now.
No one has bothered to
board up the windows.
There are five cans of
Campbell's tomato soup
on the top shelf in one.
The other was used by
the Centennial Committee
four years ago last month.
They published a book
complete with pictures
showing modern granaries,
pivot irrigation systems,
giant tractors and combines,
fertilizer and chemical stores.
That was near the end.
In the beginning of the book
there were photographs
of families and neighbors
working together on the land.

Milo Field Goodbye

Adopted daughter of the Plains,
bare knees in rough brown clods,
she takes between long tapered white
fingers a single stalk of sumac red
sorghum, feels the hardness of its
seeds, presses it firmly against her lips.

After two years on this prairie
she has come to know the wind
as her handmaiden, the grass as
second mother, milo and corn as
lovers, their fall colored leaves rushing
through her garments like cyclones,

the peaceful after storm freshness
of wet fields, smell of green and
wild plums, ripening, responding
to the planter's touch, nearing
harvest, the sound of cricket,
mourning dove, hawk and coyote.

She caresses the milo against
her cheek until she is content
then makes a small furrow in the soil
and covers it with slow easy motions
until it disappears from sight.

Tomorrow she will be on the outbound plane.

In Lincoln, Nebraska, with Carl Jung and Robert Service at Midnight

I was an iceberg
floating across the Bering Strait.
The 360° sun was unbearable
but I refused to melt.
Amundsen flew over
in his dirigible.
It was noon
and he tossed his orange peelings over the side,
missing me by inches.
Sharks tried each one
then spat it out.
I can still see the peelings
gliding along under their
pale clammy bellies.
I floated south
past Seward and Nome,
encountered seven whales,
I'm not sure what kind.
They seemed lethargic,
meandered off west,
toward Anadir.
I heard an engine and
Amelia Earhart landed
on the long smooth surface
of my northeast corner.
It was her fortieth birthday.
She drank pink champagne,
sang in harmony with a sea-lion,
then left abruptly,
tipping her wings

three times
heading into the sun,
fifty feet off the water.
Lindbergh came in,
Byrd,
Will Rogers and Wylie Post.
I saw them all,
heard them speak,
and they were gone.
It was off the
tip of the Aleutian chain,
caught in the Kuroshio Extension
that I heard the kamikaze cry
but they didn't come in.
It made the polar bears nervous.
They huddled together like kittens.
The currents pushed me
into the Gulf of Alaska.
A topsail schooner and a jackass-barque,
both running full,
slid by to starboard.
Young gold miners who
had not yet seen a mine
blinked at my reflection
off the water.
I went full circle
in the west wind currents,
touching the edge
of Kodiak Island
as I came around.

Hundreds of grizzly bears
were in the water
feasting on salmon
that turned into rainbows
under the rays of the midnight sun.
I heard a sandhill
crane dance and saw the Canadians;
the geese were low,
announcing their arrival
with golden horns borrowed from Leif Erickson.
When I came to the south
end of the circle,
a California current grabbed me
and I began to melt,
but I lasted all the way to Panama
before I vanished.
As vapor I went north
with my sisters and brothers
up into the Gulf of Mexico
where I saw Sam Houston
riding a big chestnut mare through Corpus Christi.
He was looking for Sor Juana Inés de la Cruz.
I floated over towards Laredo,
up through San Antonio then El Paso
where I turned into rain.
West Texas was appreciative
and the small part of me that
didn't soak into the parched earth
ended up in the Rio Grande.

The Old Man and the Sea

I saw it again tonight
only this time it was
Anthony Quinn not
Spencer Tracy as
the old man.
Somebody played
Hemingway
with one of those
strange drinking women
who just kind of hang
out and bitch because
he can't write.
It was sponsored by
General Motors who
came in about
every ten minutes with
a three minute commentary
about what is good for
America
claiming responsibility
for cleaning up the
environment and all
the other wonderful
things they have done
for the world and
the old man
returns with the
skeleton after the sharks
get through. Hemingway
never comes to see the
grandkids and Hadley,

Pauline and Martha,
his first, second and
third wives, are woven
in and out of the story.
Fourth wife, Mary
is somewhere else
while Ernest sits
at the bar trying to decide
if it works best to write:
man can be destroyed
but not defeated or man
can be defeated but
not destroyed.
I wonder which
it was in his mind
at the moment he
pulled that trigger
in Ketchum, Idaho.
Then I make myself
some tea and watch
the rest of *The Old Man
and the Sea* with Jake
my blue heeler dog.

Isaac

For a moment the father looked upon the face of his son, then turned trembling away.

Abraham viewed the deep sleep of his son, who had nervous seizures and often twitched in his sleep. The boy had suffered since birth and Abraham had often wished him dead but now that the time was near he was unsure. There was Sarah, Hagar and Ishmael to consider. Had he really heard the voice or was it senility? He was over a hundred years old after all. How could he be sure? He often heard voices that made no sense. It was time. He awakened the boy and after he was dressed they walked a ways out into the wilderness about a half hour from home. The boy tied the blindfold at Abraham's request and Abraham bound the boy's wrists with a long cloth turban. They had often played these games before. Then the turban slipped from the eyes of the hand bound boy and he saw the raised dagger in his father's shaky hand. No, said the boy, who loved the old man more than anything. Father, Mother has told you over and over not to play with knives. You might hurt somebody or even yourself. Give me the knife, Father. Abraham dropped the knife slowly and looked at the ground as Isaac untied his own wrists and removed the makeshift blindfold. Let us return to the house, Father. Mother will be worried and it is time for your nap. The boy took the knife and placed it back in the sheath. Slowly the old man and the boy walked back to the house where the others waited. Has the old man been talking to God again? Hagar asked. Leave him alone, Isaac said.

"Grandpa Quayle by 1922 Cadillac in Yellowstone"

The Day Comes

I read in Mardena's class
And she had the students respond
He wasn't what I expected one said
He was just like my Grandpa

The day comes
When our self-perception
Meets the reality of the way others perceive us
But I suppose her grandpa was young looking
Handsome and wise beyond his years

Just because it comes is no reason we have to accept it
All the success in the world is nothing more than fire
        glazed pottery
Molded from self-delusive clay

To those who believe

there is genuinely something to be learned
but what it is you'll never know, you who
are speeding towards death knowing there are other
deaths, other rooms where transparent coffins
are strewn about like dirty clothes in a
teenager's room. The little deaths. The
sneaky ones that come as ghosts in the night
and awake you with your heart pounding
and for a moment you wonder who is by your
side. So you put your cold against that warmth
and sleep comes but not as quickly as you wish.

White mustangs and white buffalo run through
your dreams. Comanche attack you in the Alamo.
You are Sacagawea and Jim Colter, Hugh Glass,
crippled by that grizzly bear, S. E. Hollister
with your hand gone, and Jim Beckworth,
risking your life for gold and the chief's daughters.
You are Brigham Young and George Q. Cannon,
stealing wives and daughters of Born Agains
and Catholics. Annie Oakley, Mae West, and Jackie Onassis.
You are all sixty-five Hatfields and McCoys
killed in the feud and you came to America from
East Europe through Ellis, greeted the statue in 1920.

Kilroy was here. Rosie the Riveter. Bigfoot.
The Furry Collar. The Ghostly Hitchhiker. Captain
John Smith and Pocahontas. Miles Standish and
Priscilla. Morton's Merry Mount. The Witches
of Salem. Rip Van Winkle meeting the gnome.
The Ten Lost Tribes. The Amish, with hex signs
on your barns to warn off witches. You trade in

slaves and tobacco. Sir Walter Raleigh. Jean
Nicolet, donning your oriental robes before you
enter Wisconsin. Noble Savage. Gougou monster.
The loop-garou will exact a heavy price from you.
White Voodoos hold candlelight vigils by your bed.
Hopi snake dancers, yellow = North, red = South,
white = East, green = West, will return you to
the Sun. The Mezcla Man will guard your gold.
You captains brave and bold, hear my cry, hear
my cry, my name is Captain Kidd, God's laws I
did forbid. Walk the plank, Gasparilla, Jean Lafitte,
Anne Bonney and Mary Read. Keep pistols, muskets
and cutlass clean and fit for service. No boys or
women. If a man be caught seducing any of the
latter, having carried her to sea disguised, he
shall suffer death. The Spirit of '76. Vermonters
saw the great white stallion, Ethan Allen returned

to those who believe.

Sancho Panza and the McDonald's Happy Meal

Listen to me, Dapple, we have come up
from the dark realms into the light of the
sun and not once since I became governor
of Barataria have I had my belly full, until
today, under this glorious yellow arch, the
symbol of my kingdom.

My name is Don Quixote and I assist the
dead as well as the living. Tell me who
you are for I am astounded by what I hear.

I'm Sancho Panza, and I've found my true
government, here, in this little box with a
clown's face. The ass began to bray so
loudly that the yellow arch swayed to the
unyielding sound.

That is prime witness, dear Sancho. Wait
for me; I'll hasten off to the duke's castle,
which is hard by, and get people to pull
you out of the pit where your sins, doubtless,
have cast you.

Make no haste, I pray you, sir, and for God's
sake do not come back quick, for I can't bear
being rescued until I've gorged myself with
enough fat and cholesterol to gag a hyena.

Never fear, Sancho, that's how all bad governors
should come out of their governments, just as
the sinner comes out of his deep abyss, fat,
disgusting, prone to an early heart attack, and
with a list as long as my lance of dead creatures
tied to his conscience with a nylon rope. Eat on,
brave fool. I shall return, forthwith.

I entered this government naked and naked
I shall walk away, albeit two hundred pounds
heavier. Ah, you are back, sir, and I am back
in your service. I ate six happy meals in fear
and trembling that you would not return and
at least I got my belly full.

Bellies plural looks more like it. O courageous
Sancho, let us get on to Saragossa. Perhaps we
will arrive there in time for the dedication
of the new yellow arch.

Come, Dapple, missing that event is too horrible
to contemplate. Wait up, Don Quixote, my steed,
though long and lean, has an attitude problem
and if it doesn't improve soon he's going to
become a happy meal for some other brave
and errant knight. On Dapple! Save thyself!

Imagine

Imagine if all the golf courses in America
    were turned into communal vegetable gardens.
All the private lawns
    turned into private vegetable gardens.
Each family
    owning one small car for transportation.
Every person
    having enough to eat before going to bed.
Every person
    knowing they have a bed.
Every farmer
    living on the land he farms.
All the food
    without additives and preservatives.
The cancer rate
    dropping every year.
Every citizen
    having free medical service.
Every town
    with a viable main street community.
People
    not having to live in cities.
Trading
    with each other on a local level.
Knowing
    the money would stay in the community.
A society
    not based on the profit motive.
Water
    that is clean and pure.

Air
> that is clean and unpolluted.

Families
> not broken up by industry.

Families
> not broken up by the military.

Religions
> not based on the profit motive.

War
> as a forgotten concept.

Enough
> of everything to last ten thousand years.

People
> not wanting to own, control, or use it up.

Quayle Expeditions *1972-75*

List of Illustrations

The following illustrations are used by permission and/or are part of family photo collections. All rights reserved.

Front cover photo: "Bruce in Upset," Bob Jones
Back cover photos: "The Flip," Jay Healy
i   "Floating the Colorado River," Amil Quayle, 2003, paper collage
ii   Amil Quayle portrait, 1974, Shelley Brown
xi   "Old Boatmen"
2   Grand Canyon National Park Museum Collection #GRCA 14768 (detail), John Wesley Powell, second Colorado expedition
6   Grand Canyon National Park Museum Collection #17329 John Wesley Powell, F. Dellenbaugh reflected in the Green River, May, 1871
7   Shorty Burton
12   Boatman asleep
14   Julie Thomson, photo
16   Grand Canyon National Park Museum Collection #16954 Mary Jane Colter, view south from Phantom Ranch (circa 1932)
18   Amil Quayle, paper collage
22   Tom Meyers, 2009, graphite drawing
27   Quayle family house
29   Tom Meyers, 2009, graphite drawing
31   1930 Model A
33   Tom Meyers, 2009, graphite drawing
37   Amil's father and Boy Scouts, Yellowstone Park
38   Cheddy Quayle, June, 1953
45   Lincoln Schoolhouse, St. Anthony, Idaho
46   Amil Quayle, mixed media
52   "Grandpa died in this sheepcamp"
56   Julie Thomson, photo
57   "Uncle Duff & Bill Severe: World Famous Saddlemakers"
58   Grand Canyon National Park Museum Collection #17262 R. A. Muller engraving, "Running a Rapid"
67   "Amil & Sister," Julie Thomson
68   Ernie Quayle with ponies
70   "Hungarian colt, $5,000 as a 2 yr. old"
77   Robert D. Thomson, photo
79   Robert D. Thomson, photo
81   Tom Meyers, 2009, graphite drawing
86   "1947 International," Amil Quayle
91   Amil Quayle, mixed media
104   Grandpa Quayle, 1922 Cadillac, Yellowstone
107   "Hiking the Narrows," Amil Quayle, 2003, paper collage
111   Quayle Expeditions, 1972-75